Hunter's Voices • Edited by Alan Riach

Patrick - McDiarmid + Burns Lit
self sustaining verse/ cabaret
conversation + dialogue.
contemporary - diff kinds of poems.

HUNTER'S VOICES

Poems from The Hunterian Collection
at the University of Glasgow

The Hunterian Poems Volume 3 • *Edited by Alan Riach*

STEWED RHUBARB

Published in 2024
by Stewed Rhubarb Press
Tarland, Aberdeenshire

www.stewedrhubarb.org

Poetry and other text copyright remains with
the respective writers; images copyright of
The Hunterian collection unless otherwise noted

Cover graphic by Sara Julia Campbell
Inspired by the plans for the original Hunterian
Museum designed by William Stark
www.sajuca.com

ISBN: 978-1-910416-37-2

Printed by Imprint Digital, UK

Contents

9 Foreword · Mungo Campbell
11 Hunter's Voices: An Introduction · Alan Riach
27 Acknowledgements
      28 / Joan Eardley, *The Cornfield*

· · ·

ONE: THE FOREST FLOOR
      32 / Sir David Young Cameron, *Affrick*
33 The Forest Floor · Alan Riach

· · ·

TWO: THE TREMBLING COLLECTION
      38 / Thornwood figures
39 Museum: mirror-written · Gerrie Fellows
      41 / Memel kettle drum
42 E.1, or Queen Mother · Samuel Reilly
      43 / Allan Ramsay, *William Hunter*
44 Home · Jeda Pearl
      46 / Barkcloth (Kiokio)
47 The Hunterian · Lindsay Macgregor
48 Thylacine · John Purser
      49 / Thylacine
50 H(a)unt the museum · Jeda Pearl
      51 / Interior: The Hunterian Museum

THREE: ELEMENTALS: INTERSTELLAR SPACE, EARTH, FIRE, WATER

      54 / Fragment of pallasite
55   Iron No. 1 · Stewart Sanderson
      61 / Cinnabar specimen
62   Bascart / Cinnabar · Marcas Mac an Tuairneir
      66 / Blue faience figure of Harpocrates
67   Harpocrates · Stewart Sanderson
      68 / The High Possil meteorite
69   Traces · David Kinloch
      69 / Monument dedicated to the High Possil meteorite at place of fall
70   Vertebrata (Knorpelfische) – Rays · Ian Stephen
      71 / Fish-hook (Matau)
      72 / Kava bowl (Nelcau-Amon)
73   The Nelcau at The Huntarian · Hannah Lavery
      74 / Francis Campbell Boileau Cadell, *Iona, North End*
75   Peploe to Cadell · Ian Stephen

    · · ·

FOUR: CREATION: WOMBS OF LIFE & DEATH

      78 / The child in the womb in its natural situation
79   Uterus in the Fifth Month Opened, Showing the Membranes and the enclosed foetus · Samuel Tongue
80   In Utero · Anne Frater
84   There's a Hole in the News the Size of Poetry · Jane Goldman
      88 / Unit tray of Blood-red longhorn beetles
89   Insects in the woods of Caledon · Alan Riach
      93 / Drawer of British moths and caterpillars

FIVE: POINTS OF VANTAGE

      96 / John Cunningham, *Wet Haystack*

97   The Trees · Alan Riach

      98 / Alan Davie, *Sea Devil's Watchtower*

99   In Alan Davie's Paintings · Liz Lochhead

      100 / Figure of Buddha

101   John Anderson's Buddha · Colin Bramwell

      101 / Buddha's hand

      102 / James McNeill Whistler, *Brown and Gold: Self-Portrait*

103   JMW · Ian Stephen

· · ·

SIX: ITEMS

106   Head of a Young Woman · Lynn Davidson

      107 / Alison Watt, *Head of a Young Woman*

      110 / Model 'Newcomen' steam engine

111   After Newcomen's Engine · Lindsay Macgregor

      112 / Sir Francis Legatt Chantrey, *James Watt (1736–1819)*

113   The Statue of James Watt · Bashabi Fraser

      114 / John Knox, *The Nelson Monument Struck by Lightning*

115   Òraid air an dàrna, air neo math dh'fhaoidte an treas nochdadh, de Cholbh Nelson / Speech on the second, or maybe third, unveiling of Nelson's Column · Peter Mackay

      117 / John Scougall, *John Knox*

118   Mittens · Em Strang

      119 / Mittens

      120 / Woven bag

121   A bag for magic stones · Richard Price

SEVEN: ARTICLES OF FAITH

       124 / Duncan Shanks, *Fragments of Memory*

125 Source · Liz Lochhead

       127 / Duncan Shanks, *Looking up a Gulley and Scree, Tinto*

128 Still Life and Rosechatel wi You · Lesley Benzie

       129 / Francis Campbell Boileau Cadell, *Still Life and Rosechatel*

       130 / Tombstone of Flavius Lucianus

131 Inscriptions · Gerrie Fellows

       132 / Egidius van Tilborch, *Interior with a Music Party*

       132 / A mass-produced Neapolitan mandolin

133 Chaff · Peter McCarey

134 Articles of Faith · David Kinloch

       135 / William Shaw, *A Galic and English dictionary*

       136 / Alexander Moffat, *Àird an Dòchais / The Compass of Hope*

137 The Water of Hope · Alan Riach

    · · ·

139 Biographies

Foreword · Mungo Campbell

It is almost ten years since Deborah Bennett, then Chair of the Friends of The Hunterian, suggested that it would be a good idea to commission a series of poems inspired by paintings in The Hunterian's collection. The initial ambition was to offer an encounter between words and pictures, the social experience of a promenade among the pictures of an art gallery, accompanied not by music but by the words of some of Scotland's finest contemporary poets.

Those events were a great success. The first group of poems was published, and followed by a second, this time themed on objects selected from the wider museum collections at The Hunterian.

Both projects were masterminded and edited by Alan Riach, who made equally significant poetic contributions to each book. Almost before the second volume appeared, he was suggesting that a third collection might offer fruitful ground for something rather different. The result is indeed a departure, one that reflects less on individual objects and works of art as autonomous acts of making or collecting but rather questions the many and complex intersections of intention, of means and of ends through which things have arrived, and still arrive in museum collections. These questions have been asked by the people who visit museums for rather longer than institutions such as The Hunterian have frequently acknowledged. We are all asking them now.

On occasion, such inquiry can appear challenging to institutions. As Riach reminds us in his introduction, curiosity engendered through the process of inquiry intrinsically embodies a sense of optimism. The multiple challenges set us, their readers, by the poets represented in this third collection of Hunterian poems do not necessarily propose accompanying answers. They prompt further inquiry, however. In doing so, they suggest that

Riach's 'optimism of curiosity' situated at the very heart of collections such as The Hunterian's must be counted among the most valuable assets enjoyed by museums as contemporary institutions.

One by one, each poet reminds us of this and, in offering these works, every one of these poems represents a priceless gift from them to The Hunterian.

Thank you.

Hunter's Voices: An Introduction · Alan Riach

Some years ago, I edited two books of *The Hunterian Poems*, the first of poems to paintings in the Hunterian Art Gallery at the University of Glasgow (2015), the second of poems to objects from the Hunterian Museum (2017), each with facing-page illustrations. This is the third volume in that series. It departs from the first two by focusing less on specific objects and paintings and more on a series of themes, ideas and questions, an extended and multi-faceted enquiry into The Hunterian collection as a whole, what it is, where it came from, what it cost, who pays the price, what its value is, how it helps, what it means, and what its future might be.

Considering these themes with reference to any particular object, objects, painting, paintings, artist and artists, was the invitation I sent to a range of poets whose work I especially like and admire. There were two criteria that apply also to the works of art and literature that I go back to, in whose company I find certain kinds of truth: you learn from them, and they give pleasure. I asked the poets to compose with the priority of enquiry and judgement prompted by the themes and questions, and to let that come through in their writing.

It was impossible to be completely prescriptive and I saw no point in narrowing the prompt further to begin with, but the more I thought about it, certain aspects of the project became clear, to embody what was once said of Edwin Morgan, that he possessed 'the intrinsic optimism of curiosity'. I hope this book follows that priority.

The criteria I set myself for the poems were the same as those for the previous two volumes: (1) There had to be poems in Gaelic, Scots and English, the three principle languages in which Scottish literature has been composed for millennia. (2) There had to be good representation of women as well as men. (3) And there had to be a range of poetic forms. There were a few stipulations about length: an epic was not what I wanted and two lines might not be long enough (though it could be). I was imagining a poem on one or two or maximum three pages, so there's room for succinctness but there's also space to follow an argument through. Poets almost always know what the scale of the poem will be when they're underway with it.

My notes for the 'Themes and Ideas' were simply suggestions. I asked the poets who responded to feel free to make use of them or not. This list of 21 headings serves now as an indication of themes and ideas that, to a greater or lesser extent, are pursued and explored in the poems. It introduces the book's substance, but the poets have gone in whatever directions they wanted to take. Imagination is always at work in their forms of address, in whatever imagery comes into play, in the structures of the poems, and in their tones of voice or angles of approach. I couldn't have predicted these, even had I wished to.

1 · The Collector
William Hunter himself (1718–83), his life, what 'collecting' meant for him or means more generally. Other individuals in The Hunterian: Allan Ramsay (1713–84), Joshua Reynolds (1723–92), Lord Kelvin (1824–1907), JD Fergusson (1874–1961).

2 · Appropriation and Colonialism
The political history of appropriation – theft, one might say, in the context of imperial expansion and colonial occupation; neo-colonialism; post-colonialism. The international fact with reference to the British Empire (and Scotland's participation in that, willing and enthusiastic or unwilling and reluctant, engagement with it or repudiation of it, leading it or becoming its subject

and victim). And other empires: the theme is really a universal structure of violence, the enforcement of power.

3 · Knowledge
How knowledge is constructed, gained, built, even upon material and goods that may have been tainted by appropriation – or theft. Materials that may have been lost or destroyed, kept safe in a museum for future generations to use in the accumulation of knowledge. What might that knowledge be used for in the longer term? For whose gain or benefit? And in the shorter term? Catalogues and codification. Race, ethnicity, language. The body. Communication.

4 · Representation
The idea of seeing closely, representing cultures not your own, of speaking for others or on behalf of others, sometimes things or creatures that do not have a voice of their own, or that have no voice in the language of the Collection. For example, what would that lump of deep-sea coral say? What would it sound like? (Gerda Stevenson already answered that question in a poem in a previous collection.) Or that map? Or that sarcophagus? Or the woman in that painting?

5 · Acquisition
How were such things acquired? What stories are there in the acquisition of objects? Who acquired them, where and when? The acts of acquisition? And their historical and political contexts? And the persons involved?

6 · Inheritance
Family inheritance. The inheritance of a culture. The inherited files of history: Celtic, Roman, Norse, Anglophone, Global? What

have we inherited from seas and oceans, earthly continents and archipelagos? And from Outer Space? The personal, familial and close, and the interstellar space or inter-cosmic space around us. Elemental realities: air, fire, water, earth.

7 · The Armour of Protection
What is armour? What is it for? Defence in conflict, protection of one or many kinds. Uniformity can be protection. Especially in an attack. The paradox of common purpose and individual exceptions. Vulnerability and suppression. Borders and their ambiguities.

8 · The Vulnerability of Insight
Perception as tender. Strength of conviction built out of close seeing. The eye as an instrument of measurement and sympathy. The proximity of violence. I remember a Chinese School of Botany where students studied plants by learning how to draw them. Art as the means to develop scientific knowledge.

9 · The Museum
What is it? What is it for? Who is it for? What does it contain? How do we make use of it? How do we make sense of it? How might it make people act?

10 · The Library
What is it? What is it for? Who is it for? What does it contain? How do we make use of it? How do we make sense of it? How might what we find there make people act? Systems and technologies of knowledge. In Shakespeare's time, there were about 2,000 books in print and in the early 21st century, there are more than 15 million books available online. How to select? If censorship these days means flooding all channels of communication with more and

more information, most of it irrelevant and misleading, effectively an accumulation of decoys to fool people, then it follows that knowing what to ignore is a crucial skill. Knowing how to disqualify falsehood is still the priority. The word 'library' as metaphor and historical reality: its application.

11 · The Gallery
What is it? What is it for? What does it contain? How do we make use of it? How do we make sense of it? The word 'gallery' as metaphor and historical reality: its application. Specific engineers, scientists, experimenters.

12 · Portraits and Landscapes
Generic art forms: how do they work? In complementarity? Or one at a time: what does a portrait tell you? What does a landscape tell you? A lot of 19th-century Scottish landscape painting developed from scene-painting in theatres. How does theatricality work in portraits and landscape paintings? The quality of hauntedness, in faces or bodies, in contours and terrain. How are specific geographical territories mapped by perspectives? How about generational identities in portraits? How about specific artists?

13 · The Visible (The External)
What can be seen, measured, quantified, held in shifting perspectives, understood through colour, texture, shape, dynamic form, inter-relationally, so forth.

14 · The Invisible (The Internal)
The unseen, the body's internal structures and flow, vessels and tensions and torts. Spine and bone and marrow. Mind. The spirit. What moves the clay and makes it grow tall.

15 · Fashion and Health
What we wear, how we wear it. Clothes and physique. How we walk or sit. How we behave in company. How we arrange our cutlery, if we do. How we touch each other, physically, as sentient beings, or across space: into the mind through the ears, into the heart through the eyes.

16 · Birth and Death (of Individuals / of Cultures)
Mortality is fact: individual persons, languages, ecosystems, cultures, civilisations, species, structures, empires, planets, stars, cosmological identities. Does self-consciousness mean that we must treat knowledge differently? And intuition?

17 · Currency and Coins
Literally, the coin collection. But any 'commerce' of 'exchange' is the dynamic of the whole thing. The Collection itself is a momentary pause with all that it contains. (And in constant dialogue and exchange with other Collections internationally.)

18 · Meteors, Fossils and Stone
Things from outer space: minerals, colours, shapes, sharp edges, these arrivants. And the residuals, in earth, on earth, what has accrued, ores, deep time: James Hutton's perception.

19 · Flora and Fauna
Birds and beasts and everything else: fish and insects, butterflies and snakes, bacteria and mammals, reptiles, 'deformities', shells and corals, forests and deserts, inhabitants and nomads, whatever we might call 'ecological balance'. Do any wild creatures die of old age? Loss. Extinction. Defence. Protectiveness. Violence. The Rainbow Warrior.

20 · 'To make you see'
As Joseph Conrad said his purpose in his writing was, ultimately. Maybe, also, to make you hear? To listen as well as to look? Or 'to make you see' as in 'understand', which is to hear deeply, to taste, to trace the scent, where the tracks connect. Where understanding comes from. And sympathy. (The five senses in the sequence of their human acquisition: sound, touch, taste, sight, smell.) Music comes before seeing, and seeing comes before words, but words are both seeing and music. Different things, connected, partial, in touch.

21 · Control and the uncontrollable – and magic
What's the wild? What's wilderness? That which cannot be controlled. There is wildness that means risk, for real: it can kill you, and there's a wildness you can make comfortable to be in. You can domesticate it. That's how the sublime becomes the picturesque. Wonder is the other side of horror; both can be tuned stale by over-exposure, over-explanation, over-familiarity. Control is the index, the catalogue, the inventory, the dictionary, the encyclopaedia. That's the risk of the ultimate index. The Enlightenment is its birthplace and the Museum its mausoleum. But there is something else here: serendipity. The accidentalism of unpredicted discovery. Such discoveries: you can make them in museums, in libraries, in galleries, in books, and when they work, they're magic. Magic is what cannot be explained.

None of these, I suggested, should be considered exclusive or totally prescriptive and most of them overlap or connect in one way or another. The idea was to be thinking about these themes or ideas, or some of them, and bringing in imagery and reference to paintings or museum items from the collection itself. And there was no ambition for the book to be exhaustive in its treatment of these themes and ideas. It's a poet's collection of other poets' poems, so it's full of sharp edges, unexpected endings or starts, and following Edwin Morgan's advice once again, leaves symmetry to the cemeteries.

The result was as brilliant as I had hoped for and as it had to be, unpredicted. The book is a showcase of a wide range of contemporary Scottish poets and their poetry, as well as a showcase and interrogation of the Hunterian collection itself.

Bringing the poems into some sort of readable order was the final problem posed by the prospect of the book's publication. With such a diversity of subjects and so many different kinds of poem, it would be a chaos without at least an attempt to indicate some governing sense of priorities and sequence, not to fix and locate but to let the currents running between and across poems be visible, or a little more palpable.

In the end, after much reading and rereading and thinking, I settled on a kind of configuration. As with previous Hunterian collections, I left it until the poems had come in before considering the question, what hasn't been written about? What areas of the collection have been left undisturbed? There are almost literally innumerable items, but there is a deep current, I think, to do with nature and the climate crisis which the world of western exploitation, the world as it has emerged from the Enlightenment and the rise of Empire, the world in which The Hunterian collection evolved, has brought us into. And this prompted my own contributions, at specific points in the book, beginning with the floor of the Caledonian Forest, the Great Wood.

In fact, the frontispiece, Joan Eardley's 'The Cornfield' sets the tone: a vision of terrestrial nature, a Scottish landscape, but also a depiction of cultivated nature, a farmed field, a territory of transformation. This is not a nomadic but a settled world. And yet the energy it depicts is nature unsettled, always in movement, and that's visible, palpable, in the colours and shapes on the canvas. Let that stand for an opening into this strand of the book's enquiry. And a special thanks here to Duncan Lockerbie, the book's designer, who has taken colours from the Eardley masterpiece for the colours of the dividing section titles. If there's a coherence to this book's arguments in words there is also a coherence to its colour schemes and all its long connections.

We begin with '**The Forest Floor**' and a literal description of a reality of birds, small animals, trees, flora, fauna, insects, microscopic nutrients, a place of life regenerating through death and decay. What can simply be seen beyond the windowpane. And this should keep the imagination in touch with the reality: the life of our nation's first inhabitants, fungi, flowers, vegetation, animal life of essential minuteness, each tiny creature seeing and sensing and understanding as it could, through compound eyes and exoskeletal structures. It's a world of inhuman movement and trajectories beyond our practice. There is so much still to learn from these. We'll return to them.

The title for Part Two is taken from a specific exhibition, '**The Trembling Museum**', except here that 'trembling' is felt in the collection as a whole, and in the Collector, William Hunter, and his fellow-Collectors and Contributors and Curators. Gerrie Fellows's 'Museum: mirror-written' and Samuel Reilly's 'E.1, or Queen Mother' respond (among other things) to objects from that exhibition, a man, woman and baby on a moped from Nigeria and a drum from Ghana, Africa, but their poems are not limited to the focus of single objects. And Jeda Pearl's 'Home' and 'H(a)unt the Museum' address questions about the museum itself and the vocabulary, disposition and authority used and assumed to present it.

It's important to note that the excerpt that inspired Jeda's text in the found poem 'Home' was reviewed by The Hunterian as it featured problematic perspectives and terminology now understood to be discriminatory. Jeda's poem exemplifies the liability of this and commemorates historical formulations which she rightly questions and rejects, and which The Hunterian has recognised and addressed. Lindsay Macgregor's 'The Hunterian' annotates items: 'sectioned / selves', 'dioramas of loss' and 'the foetus of enlightenment', 'poised for delivery. Then dissection.' The Polynesian barkcloth that goes with it is only one sample of something whose life took place beyond the confines of the rooms we walk through here. And even more comprehensively, John Purser's 'Thylacine' describes the Tasmanian Wolf which is itself a composite creation, a creature assembled from representatives of a species now consigned to the oblivion of extinction – and yet preserved in the museum, and in the poem, alongside the poet's comprehension of its meaning.

Part Three brings in '**Elementals: Interstellar Space, Earth, Fire, Water**': the component parts of our reality, beginning acknowledgement of the blow-ins, immigrants, interstellar space travellers, meteorites, and what they might generate on earth, new configurations and combinations of humanity's identities. Beginning with Stewart Sanderson's extraordinary assemble-it-yourself handbook for making new poems, 'Iron No. 1', prompted by the Pallas Meteorite, and offering a couple of examples of how that might work. Marcas Mac an Tuairneir's 'Bascart' / 'Cinnabar' takes the same theme further in a different format altogether. The shape of the poem predicates its layout on the page, differing from others, a sit must. Stewart Sanderson returns with 'Harpocrates': 'what's waiting between your words' from Egyptian and Roman periods through the long history of languages and humanity trying to deal with changes encapsulated in a small figurine, 'last reports': too many 'truth commissions [...] much redacted'. And David Kinloch, in 'Traces' brings the High Possil Meteorite back to its Glasgow provenance, which leads to Ian Stephen's locating the internal and external realities – from the fossil of the Bearsden shark to Polynesian fish-hooks: 'achieved shapes / as various as ballads'. Stephen comments: 'We're lost in the looking, / more so, in the trying.' Yet try we must, and he goes on in the next poem, looking at one of Cadell's great Iona paintings, a depiction of a geographical physicality where a spiritual dimension grown through history remains undeniable, in the air through which we see, and in its recorded actuality. These are elemental things, indeed.

Part Four, '**Creation: Wombs of Life & Death**' concentrates first on a single, controversial, deeply disturbing object that has compelled more than one poet to address its history and lasting significance: the Gravid Uterus, the definitive centre of the 'Curating Discomfort' enquiry. It is there for good and bad, made out of priorities we might find reprehensible, repugnant, appalling, and maintained for good reasons, commemorating something so awful that it must not be forgotten. The object is the focus of poems by Samuel Tongue, 'Uterus in the Fifth Month Opened, Showing the Membranes and the enclosed foetus' and Anne Frater's 'In Utero', both of them, in English and in Gaelic, with forensic objectivity and understated compassion, speculate, enquire, evoke, memorialise, and lead on towards Jane Goldman's 'There's a Hole in the News the Size of Poetry', where a different poetic form allows a different kind of speculative enquiry to go forward at a different pace. Human sensitivity and physical creativity and the construction of poetry itself are both imbricated in each of these poems, deeply and subtly. There is no lack of compassion or judgement but there is a profound commitment in all of them to this principle of creativity.

And this is where I wanted to return to the Caledonian Forest and the insect life abundant within it. The insect collection in the Hunterian is an extensive resource but rarely the subject of poems. I thought that perhaps, by looking at it within an overall narrative implication of life and death, regeneration and creativity, what's most vulnerable today and what remains most valuable, I might offer an emphasis worth making here, something unpredicted to put beside the Gravid Uterus. This poem returns us to that creative potential I mentioned beginning with Eardley's 'The Cornfield' frontispiece and the ever-moving world of nature we can see beyond the windowpane.

Part Five, '**Points of Vantage**' took as its premise Liz Lochhead's *tour de force* poem on Alan Davie's paintings, and particularly 'Sea Devil's Watchtower'. The almost abstract use of the Scots language in the poem, its sheer exhilaration of its sound, matches precisely the brilliant colours and quasi-abstract vision of the painting, yet both ask questions and draw immediately from the realities of their reference points. What can we see through – or rather, *with* – 'An ee / an open ee' not only when we're looking *at*, but also perhaps when we're looking out *from*, that Watchtower? What would be the best place to see from, the best point of vantage? I wanted to think of that with reference to John Cunningham's painting, 'Wet Haystack', which I've known for most of my life. John was my uncle and returning to the University of Glasgow in 2001 it was a warming recognition when I located the painting on long-term loan, hanging in the Principal's Lodging. The painting itself suggests different points of view within itself, from where you stand, from above looking down from the blue patch of sky, from the foreground context of high, wet hay and grass. In a sense, it rhymes, or chimes, with the colours and shapes of Eardley's 'The Cornfield'.

Such echoes and traces and affinities are there throughout the book, and I'm only noting a few of them as we go. But the 'points of vantage' are not only literal in landscape or personal history. They're present across cultures and religions, as Colin Bramwell shows in 'John Anderson's Buddha'. Colin wrote to me about his poem: 'There are two John Andersons behind this one; one the founder of the Andersonian institute, but also the Scottish-Australian philosopher John Anderson, theorist of "Australian realism", a school of philosophy which the poem engages with. The poem also responds to Rilke's "Archaïscher Torso Apollos", but not so explicitly that it needs an "After", I think.' I agree. Colin's poem stands on its own, but if anyone is prompted to read Rilke's poem, all to the good. Colin also noted: 'I've taken a liberty and changed the material of the sculpture from ivory/soapstone to bronze; a better prosodic fit, and bronze is the best element for the poem. I hope that's okay – I know we're meant to be responding to the originals, and I am, but in my experience I'm rarely able to be exactly faithful to the inspirations of a poem, the poem tends to take on its own form of life that doesn't always match reality perfectly...' And that too is an example of the poets taking their own liberties beyond any prescriptions.

In this poem, the Myanmar Figure of Buddha 'sets daylight free // to exhaust the eye'. The perennial conflicts remain: 'The poor will take what they can from the poorer – / you can't change that. You can't change anything.' It's a familiar consolation, and a teaching. But change does happen. There is progress, for better and worse. Ian Stephen's 'JMW' simply draws attention to Whistler's 'organisation of / legs, arms, miraculous hands.' Are those human hands, made in the painting of pigment by his actual hands, not somehow evidence of that, beyond the mighty cradle of the Buddha's hand on the previous page?

Part Six, '**Items**', returns us to poems addressing specific objects and paintings from the collection that didn't seem to fit – or want to be squeezed into – any of the other sections, and it seemed to me right and appropriate that such individual poems and images should have a space of their own. Thus Alison Watt's portrait painting, 'Head of a Young Woman', prompted Lynn Davidson's poem 'Head of a Young Woman' and Jane Goldman, following not only Alison Watt's painting but also Lynn Davidson's poem, has her own poem, 'A Face on the move', so the lines of communication, and of opening the enquiry across the arts, continue. In a different kind of commerce of communication, the Model 'Newcomen' steam engine had already prompted a poem by Jim Carruth, in *The Hunterian Museum Poems*, but here Lindsay Macgregor, in 'After Newcomen's Engine' has a different take on it again.

The whole collection comes back into view with Bashabi Fraser's 'The Statue of James Watt'. Sir Francis Leggatt's sculpture places the figure firmly within the Museum's space, but the connections cannot be predicted. The painting by John Knox, 'The Nelson Monument Struck by Lightning' was one of those left alone by the poets but which we very much wanted to include. When I asked Pàdraig MacAoidh / Peter Mackay if he might oblige us by taking it as his prompt, he responded with 'Òraid air an dàrna, air neo math dh'fhaoidte an treas nochdadh, de Cholbh Nelson' / 'Speech on the second, or maybe third, unveiling of Nelson's Column'. The humour at work here is wonderfully dark, elemental, wayward and fine, as Peter collides the artist and the Calvinist reformer and the confluence produces one of the funniest poems in the collection. It seemed only fair to include John Scougall's portrait of John Knox (the Calvinist) as well.

Em Strang, in 'Mittens', responded to a Native American / Canadian First Nations pair of mittens, and Richard Price, in 'A bag for magic stones' brought in a bag from New Caledonia, Melanesia. Em's last verse is a piercingly poignant reminder of the limitations of all our knowledge, and that's an essential point to the book, and the collection as a whole: 'Who made us? Ask the snow. / Ask the North Wind. Ask the wide land...' We all reside still, 'inside the not-knowing forever.' Acknowledging this, we can still hope for better in the day-to-day, the mundane, the quotidian realities, mittens, personal jealousies, family 'tenderness and touch', the risks and dangers, the protectiveness and sometimes the urge to yield to violence. Richard's poem rests on a kind of secular prayer, though: 'May there be a rich harvest.' A harvest of what? For whom? How should we understand that wish?

My final answer is in the last section of the book, '**Articles of Faith**'. This brings us to things we might trust in, not blindly, but surely. Liz Lochhead's 'Source' takes into view the work of Duncan Shanks, from which so many examples might have been placed for illustration here. That's because Liz's poem so deftly captures one of the 'articles of faith' that run through the book as a whole: '*the artist's work / should always speak for itself*' – well, yes, it should, but there is always, also, 'a brassy shaft of light through cloud, / the mixed blessing of a downpour'. To paraphrase: *You have to go out to go in*. The relations between the worlds of art and the objects of the Museum and Gallery and the artists' practice and the poets' poems, and exactly, truthfully, what this world is, *out there*, are at the heart of it all. And is it not the case that understanding this, not as theory or rationality or numerically verifiable data, but as lived practice, is what allows us any life at all?

In the early 21st century, the question is urgent. But if there are 'articles of faith' still worth believing in, this is where you'll find them, in paintings, poetry and music, in the languages of art. Lesley Benzie, in 'Still Life and Rosechatel Wi You' says so with vernacular immediacy: we need 'the wurkins o pure airt' to love; we need 'this backdrop o Prussian Blue' and the chair, 'bricht reid, colour saturate'. Her poem holds forth the truth of Cadell's painting in another medium, and then returns us to it with cleansed eyes. Gerrie Fellows skips us back to a tombstone from the Bar Hill Roman Fort and annotates the inscriptions on its worn sandstone, still decipherable, still to be read: 'forgotten / guessed at / come to light' as 'the laverock sings over'.

Peter McCarey's lacing together of a wooden mandolin he played himself once, with the painting by Egidius van Tilborch, 'Interior with Music Party', prompts him to question what lasts, what's chaff, what's corn, what's blown away in the world's wide winds, what's remembered, kept and used, and what it is we 'cannae mind'. And David Kinloch's poem on Wiliam Shaw's Gaelic / English Dictionary from 1780 reminds us that these questions have pertinence here and now in our own languages, our own culture and cultures, identities, positions, powers.

This is where we might find credible 'Articles of Faith'. Here is a language where the letters of the alphabet stand for the initials of trees: 'A' is for Ailm, which is Elm, to begin with. And that first letter of the alphabet is a closing connection back to the trees we've been among, the Caledonian forest floor, the woods beyond the windowpane, the forests of The Hunterian collection we've been losing ourselves in, and finding ways through, questioning, and returning from. And that's what I hope my own final poem in the book, 'The Water of Hope' might offer affirmation of: 'good hopes, these prospects: / Aspirations. Independence.'

Acknowledgements

At The Hunterian, thanks go especially to Mungo Campbell, Lee Scott, Harriet Gaston and Jeanne Robinson, for their extraordinary commitment to the whole project and many particular aspects and details of it.

We must also thank The Chancellor's Fund at the University of Glasgow for supporting the research, publication and public dissemination of this book, and our presentation of it as an ongoing method of engagement and encouragement to our students, to connect the treasures of The Hunterian, the questions the collection raises, and the answers it sometimes provides, with their fields of study, not least of literature and poetry in all its dimensions.

Thanks go to our publisher Charlie Roy and book designer Duncan Lockerbie at Stewed Rhubarb, a Scottish poetry press known for the diversity of its list and its high production values.

Access to The Hunterian collection is a permanent joy and privilege for those of us who work at the University of Glasgow, and for people within striking distance, in the west of Scotland. If you're farther away, you can begin with The Hunterian website on the Collections page: www.gla.ac.uk/hunterian/collections/

And after that, if you want to go to the Collections database for more information on each object or painting: www.gla.ac.uk/collections/

And for the University of Glasgow 'Poetry & Poetics' website recording of the launch of The Hunterian Poems: www.gla.ac.uk/schools/critical/research/researchclusters/poetryandpoetics/

Past events, readings from The Hunterian Poems, at Glasgow's Aye Write! Festival, the Lyon & Turnbull Gallery in Edinburgh, in the Hunterian Art Gallery and in the museum, and elsewhere, have been happy and curious occasions, setting good precedents for the present book.

Joan Eardley, *The Cornfield*, c.1958–62. © the Eardley estate. All rights reserved, DACS 2024.
GLAHA:43471

ONE

THE FOREST FLOOR

Sir David Young Cameron, *Affrick*, c.1880–1945. GLAHA:43428

The Forest Floor · Alan Riach

From my window, the blue sky sails
    through high Scots oaks and beech,
sycamore, ash, hawthorn and spruce,
       lights and makes shadows on
innumerable tangles of branches,
    angled, twisted, stretching horizontal,
thinning, leaning, curving down
    or thinly sloping out above their neighbours,
almost touching, slender,
    as the tall slim sturdy trunks might sway
a little, in the wind,
    or in a storm, might bend, and leaves
shiver green like flames in a flaring fire,
       but cold in the rain
or even just the early spring blue air,
       coming among them, there.

That squirrel,
    moves so fast then stops,
dead still, legs spread,
claws caught on the bark,
    then heads up, races again, and leaps
to how can it know where, or how secure,
       how pliant and connected,
how brittle or broken the next branch
         might be?
Hits safely, darts on,
up and around, into the woods,
    reappears further on, stops, still,
then moves again,
       and is gone.

There is an endless tension, day and
night. Animals and trees don't sleep.
The beasts might close their bodies down
              a while. Trees never do.
    The tension never goes away entirely.
A forest at night is dark, but never asleep.
Night creatures move and sound
in their own time, darkly, but highly awake:
the tension is acute.
     Day creatures, that squirrel,
gone elsewhere, stay fast in their proprioception:
we look on and study, can only imagine,
get into, sometimes, for a moment or two.

The wilderness things are within it, all of their lives.
Almost none of them die of old age.
Predators, invaders, diseases brought in,
        removals, destructions,
the industry mind, the numbers folk,
    the dollars talk, disrupt. Pollution spoils.
But wilderness things connect.
Trees, squirrels, birds,
       from sky to the forest floor.
Voles, mice, spiders, ants.
     and under the earth, the worms.
        And nutrients of corpses.

At dusk the crows coagulate,
    their throats fill out
        with flowing music craws,
cacophonies of polyphonic soaring
    growing massive, individuations, as the sky
gets duskier and darker and the darkness
        starts to close things down.
They gather on the branches of the tall Scots oaks
    and other trees and mass.
A Catholic conglomerate of Protestants,
and then, at one moment, they rise, flying out
of the mesh of the traps of the branches,
all in curves and angles, fast, freely –
Then in a cloud of winged black bodies, connected
        and singular, curve up and out
and into the air,
    and turn in an arc,
then bar in another,
        then over our heads
and return once again,
and then take themselves off into darkness,
and go as the sound of their crying and calling
    grows less, and then less,
        and then settles, into silence. Not silence.
And we turn, go indoors,
    to our rooms, to our beds,
        to our warming, and silence. Not silence.

TWO

THE TREMBLING COLLECTION

Thornwood figures, Southern Nigeria. GLAHM:138543

Museum: mirror-written · Gerrie Fellows

Boxes   wrapped for quarantine   6.7 kg
West Africa Ethno 720   and in reverse   boxed   mirror-written
Kenya East Africa Ethno 473   South Africa 5.8 kg
In each box what might be   what might have been
wrapped for quarantine
Do not open from one year of the above date

Memel, drum   Unknown Fante Artist, Southern Ghana
silent   yet the air in the gallery
trembles

like the shimmer of a thread on a robe
an embroidered pattern on a Babban Riga
Hausa needlework crossed with the desert's traces

or the coiled lace of cassava root paste on Adire Eleko
a cloth of root, soil, place   indigo-dyed
its colour is of ocean   the resist an erasure   the pale line
like the line of a worm in the wood of a slave ship
        an erasure and a continuity
        boxed   quarantined

        carried
        like the thread of sound
        from Africa into the Delta Blues

·

Place might be   the strike of a mattock on red earth
a ground of palm nuts rolled on wood   a shaping
from memories and divination and the present tense

a boy turns a handstand   a woman dances
a family on a moped spin dust in their wheels
Are they people in a landscape, these thornwood figures?

The tree they are made from
is timber, medicine   meetings and talk in its shade
ceiba pentandra   holed by insect, gnarled by fungi
a dwelling in place or in sound   in speech
in what is carried in the arms,

                                        on the back in the mouth

in memory

                    unwrapped

        masks and living faces
        in the black and white of the film
        in the dark and light in the gallery

Memel kettle drum, 1800–89, Southern Ghana. GLAHM:E.1

E.1, or Queen Mother · Samuel Reilly

Hunter'd had a century in the ground
Before E.1's Atlantic voyage found
An end in his museum. 'Ethnography One' –
The founding father of its type of hoard.
The unknown Fante hand that carved it called
It *memel*, or 'Queen Mother of the Band'.
Sequestered in its glass vitrine, the drum
Is silent now, its dancing days all done.

Enlightened vision foundered on the coast
Of Africa, beguiled by lure of gold.
It took an age of newly Christian zeal
To find out what these cultures were about
– if often with a view to muscling out
Gods with god, a tussle between hosts and ghosts
That echoes down to us in material
Like this: dead wood – but are the spirits well?

Remember, in its day, E.1 would govern
Ompe or *Adzewa* bands, and dancers
Limning trembling lovers' marriage feasts.
Newer *memel* drums have paint, and figures;
This example, brown all over, lingers
Longer in the mind, its patterns preserving
Gestures of the adze and with them faintest
Memories of the rhythms it has lost.

There are now thirteen hundred things marked 'E'
In the Hunterian, each a history
Of obsolescence, whether fair or forced.
Museums record the ways we cease to wear
The past, as it becomes the past, for fear
Of bungling the present – but equally
The ways we keep what we would hide too close:
A means of losing track, and tracking loss.

Allan Ramsay, *William Hunter*,
1763–66. GLAHA:44026

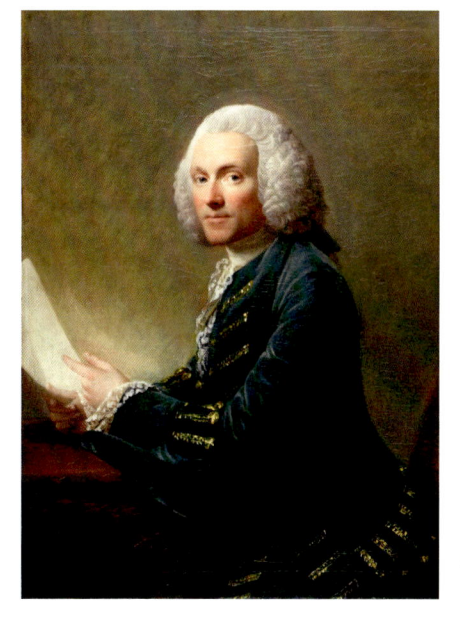

Home · Jeda Pearl

exciting natural curios
many believe objects returning are on loan
claim further donation
mission neglected
another body meticulously labelled
ethnography class
first contact home
to collect other bodies

A found poem taken from this now removed excerpt on the Hunterian's website:
'The Hunterian is home to an exciting and varied collection of both natural and artificial 'curiosities', many of which are believed to have come from the voyages of Captain James Cook. Although the ethnography collection has objects from around the world, many of the "star" objects in the collection were acquired by William Hunter from the returning Cook expeditions during the period 1771-1780. Some of these are currently on loan to the internationally acclaimed *James Cook and the Exploration of the Pacific* exhibition. The collection was further enhanced by the donation from the Rev Dr. George Turner, a Scottish missionary, in 1860. In 1888, the surviving artefacts from the neglected Andersonian Museum at Anderson's College, Glasgow, added another fine body of material, many pieces meticulously labelled. Although a relatively modest size, the quality of the ethnography collection is world class and includes many spectacular "first contact" pieces. It is also home to an outstanding body of Maori carvings, one of the world's finest earliest barkcloth collections and other bodies of unprovenanced material which are almost certainly from the Cook voyages.'

home exciting
natural curios many
believe

objects

returning
are on loan
claim
further
donation
mission
neglected
another body
meticulously labelled
ethnography class
first contact
home to
collect other bodies

Barkcloth (Kiokio), c.1700–1860, Hawaii. GLAHM:E.417/6

The Hunterian · Lindsay Macgregor

In the westernmost recess of this mind
    the founding fathers expose their sectioned
selves in bits of Polynesian barkcloth,
    lures strewn amongst imperial rubble
by the company of scotland, a hoard
    of golden nobles gawping at someone's
bottled testicles in dioramas
    of loss. The central chamber houses me-
teorites in first contact with mummies,
    gravid uteruses flayed to reveal
the foetus of enlightenment given
    national significance as a resource
cast to contain our curious nature
    poised for delivery. Then dissection.

Thylacine · John Purser

I remember you – or rather 'youse',
youse being a compilation
of skeleton, skin and skull.
I was little then, a few years out of my pouch,
my father giving me new perspectives
on the passage of time.
He lectured there: took me to the very top of the spire,
Arran visible miles away, the wind
searching alarmingly through the cast-iron spiral
staircase, the filigree of narrowing stonework.

But there was nothing so fearful as that one word, extinct.
Hard for a little boy to grasp, but with a strange allure.
Not just gone, but gone forever; and this memorial not even
individual – not that I knew that at the time. I believed
I was face to face with a reality:
a Tasmanian wolf whose thoughts
commanded its body; not some taxidermal transplantation.

I've met the construct's relatives –
Tasmanian devils in their home territory.
They have their own type of charm.
But I cannot say that I
have met a true Tasmanian human
for there are none. Extinct. Well, not quite.
Some compilations survived whose ancestors
had bred with whites.

Now in old age I gather
my library for archiving and commence
disposal of my effects, to family,
to museums. Not long to go, but it will not be
extinction. Not the real thing,
the real thing that is not, the Thylacine:
a wasteland of unrecoverable genes.

Thylacine, *(Thylacinus cynocephalus)*, Tasmania, Australia. Transferred to
The Hunterian from the Andersonian College, 1888. GLAHM:Z503

H(a)unt the museum · Jeda Pearl

'The Hunterian is home to an exciting and varied collection of both natural and artificial "curiosities".'

As I wander this warm place
through my computer screen
Am I the artefact? Or artificial
in conceding to my own romanticising
of skin stretched
across taxidermist curiosities
My eyes impaling upon impaled minibeasts
Spectating the spoils
Whitemansplained
If to discover is to uncover what
and who were already existing
What is it I am discovering?

Interior: The Hunterian Museum

THREE

ELEMENTALS: INTERSTELLAR SPACE, EARTH, FIRE, WATER

Fragment of pallasite, Russia. GLAHM:M174

Iron No. 1 · Stewart Sanderson

an analogue poetry generator

starfallen pindaric fragment	traveller from unknown worlds	tiniest sliver of the infinite
gem amidst the cosmic slag heap	messenger older than language	debris from a forgotten battle
a small piece of a larger object	adept in the science of silence	stratigraphy of homesick days

---

which has found a way to reach us	happened upon deep in the taiga	as encountered by a blacksmith
discovered by a mining foreman	studied in the tsarist academy	buffeted our way by solar winds
the same colour as a millennium	quiet like a forgotten dialect	dwelling here in our rainy city

---

it means something it came here	it has spoken to the snow leopards	it has heard the dwarf pine sigh
it was sent here for some reason	its one desire is to be accepted	it has no need of our acceptance
it fashions dreams atom by atom	it has strange truth to confess	its arrival here meant nothing

and we can do nothing but listen	since it passes understanding	if it mastered farewells early
but it will not reveal this to us	and it thinks fondly of the cold	for it has no fantasies of order
and in some ways is not unlike us	and the bird cherry confirms it	and so it presents a choice to us

———————————————

today we must look again at this	we follow it into the distances	we look at it because it loves us
we meet the future in its figure	we love it as it has endured much	we must sing it schistose peaks
we must imagine its one purpose	tomorrow we will ask a question	we have no way to know the secret

———————————————

for here too there is dialectic	revolution after revolutions	each generation will misprise
but will not be worried by it for	then fall asleep atop the stove	for so it will be at home among us
though the answer terrifies us	yet are beyond enlightenments	the reason why it has descended

whatever truth it holds within	even if time eats this away also	regardless of magnetic fields
no matter where it may move on to	to set this in its wider context	however long corroding take it
wherever its far journey began	before we consider theodicies	whoever finds themselves here

―――――――――――――

we may always have the hope that	as yet unwritten histories say	in the bleats of a sheep we learn
in the samovar steam we can read	at least one wild prophet rants	it would be most unwise to think
a half-burnt manuscript holds	it would be foolish not to think	there is an epic which finishes

―――――――――――――

it could yet become a horseshoe	some day we may reach its planet	it works so slowly on its design
each crystal is a form of prayer	it wants to be made into bullets	this is all we can ever aspire to
it emulates the ideal republic	it may never belong in our place	someone may come looking for it

Note on Method

Iron No. 1, bequeathed to the Museum by William Hunter himself, is a small fragment of the Pallas meteorite: the first to be recognised as such by science.

My 'Iron No. 1' is intended to function not as a single poem, which the reader might be expected to make their way through in a more or less linear fashion, but rather as a means whereby a potentially very large number of poems can be generated.

The reader-writer is of course free to find their way into this text in any way which makes sense to them. However, this analogue generator has been initially designed to produce poems of nine lines each. This is because the smallest repeatable three-dimensional iron lattice would be a cube comprising nine atoms. The reader-writer is, in this model, presented with nine options for each of their poem's nine lines. Each potential line has 26 letters, reflective of iron's atomic number.

It is suggested that reader-writers employ some kind of aleatory procedure to select the lines for their poems. This could involve, for example, using a nine-sided die, either via a virtual roller or a 1d10, re-rolling 10s. Or pointing at the various options until a fellow reader-writer, who is looking the other way or closing their eyes, says stop – at which point the option indicated becomes the next line. Other approaches are encouraged.

It is hoped that this combination of chance procedure and a potentially very large number of possible combinations will speak, in some way, to the enormous contingencies which, first, led the Pallas meteorite from wherever it initially came from to Siberia and, second, led Iron No. 1 to Glasgow.

Several sample poems, by no means intended to be authoritative instances, have been randomly generated and included on the following pages.

I

starfallen pindaric fragment
dwelling here in our rainy city

its arrival here meant nothing
and so it presents a choice to us
and the bird cherry confirms it

we follow it into the distances
but will not be worried by it for
before we consider theodicies
there is an epic which finishes

each crystal is a form of prayer

II

tiniest sliver of the infinite
discovered by a mining foreman

it has heard the dwarf pine sigh
and in some ways is not unlike us

we follow it into the distances

revolution after revolutions

even if time eats this away also
it would be foolish not to think
this is all we can ever aspire to

Cinnabar specimen, Slovenia. GLAHM:M9798

Bascart
Marcas Mac an Tuairneir

Sa chiad dol-seachad,
air glèidheadh air cùl glainne,
cha b' e seo bascart Idrijia,
far an robh breug-shealladh
na dhearg-chaothach
am broinn toll-dubh Antaine
is lionnach airgid-bheò, a'
sileadh sìos gu peilichean fionn-sgeulach,
làn uisge fho-thìrich.

Palenque,
far am bu stragaidh neamhnaidean
mu laighe na banrigh ruaidh,
froiseadh snàithlean a tuirc,
neadachadh sligean
's leugan-sèada a tiara,
a' fàilligeadh ma ceann
fhad 's a ghabh na mìrean sgàrlaid
ri èirigh a' bhrothaill

Mar an ceudna,
cha b' e seo bascart

Almadén,
far am bu losgadh nì talmhanta e,
a lìon cuislean, 's a losg
a thùsan bolcànach,
a' cnagadh, is guailte
an suachdain is stàilean Ioslamach e,
gus an tugadh air fallas
deòir a bhichirb, a' dìleadh
thar amar na Mara Meadhanaiche.

Giza,
far am bu shamhla trèine e,
is buinnig air an t-sìorraidheachd,
na chadal 's air fhalach
an sgòrnanan chorp spriosraichte,
sùil-chrith a phìnndeachaidh
air a shireadh le seidhcean,
a' ceumadh o àilean gu àilean
son ìocshlaint an sinnsrean.

Guizhou,
far am bu sgrìobht' e
air damh-shlinnean,
gan caochladh nan cnàmhan faidheil,
ceistean 's caileadaireachd beirmilein,
thoradh nam bruisean orra,
's na flothagan ruiteachain
glèidhte ann an sruth
fliuch na h-ince.

Nan àite, b' e an sampla seo
chaidh sgoradh mu dheireadh
a-mach à mèinn Thìr na Rèine,
a sheaghaich stòras,
sgìolta a-nis,
is gnìomhachas
a bha, aon uair, beò am Wolfstein.

Fuil dràgoin eachdraidh
air a phronnadh gu pùdar,
a chriomagan caithte
dhan àile
le cuibhle tìm.

Cinnabar
Marcas Mac an Tuairneir

Upon first encounter,
enshrined behind glass,
this was not the cinnabar
of Idrija, where hallucinations
raged inside Anthony's Shaft
and liquid quicksilver rained down
into its legendary buckets
of subterranean water.

Likewise,
this was not
the cinnabar of

Almadén,
where the vein-filling mineral
burned out its volcanic origins,
cracking, charred,
in Islamic furnaces and alembics,
until forced to sweat
its mercury tears,
seeping out across
the Mediterranean basin.

Palenque,
where, scattered with pearls,
the red queen lay,
the skein of her necklace
fraying, shells nestling into cuts
of jade,
her diadem disintegrating
around her head
as the scarlet particles took
to the swelter, rising.

Guizhou,
where, written onto ox scapula,
it transformed these
into oracle bones,
vermillion questions and
prognostications brushed on,
the ruby flecks,
suspended in the fluid
flow of ink.

This example instead,
the last hacked out
of a Rhineland mine,
signified a now depleted resource,
an industry once alive
in Wolfstein.

The dragonblood of yesteryear,
powdered down,
its fragments cast
into the ether
by the wheel
of time.

Giza,
where, symbolising strength
and victory over the eternal,
it slept, sequestered,
in the throats of the embalmed,
its quivering coagulation
sought out by sheikhs,
trekking oasis to oasis,
for the elixir of the ancients.

Blue faience figure of Harpocrates, 30 BC–AD 395, Egypt. GLAHM:D.1929.64

Harpocrates · Stewart Sanderson

I am what's waiting in between your words:
the absence of an answer to your prayer
     as well as that which gnaws
at all your music, chews the closing chords
of each performance – and when the applause
has petered out, believe me, I am there.

In my long life I've eaten languages –
spitting the date stones of Sumerian,
     Etruscan's olive pips
and some day I will do the same with this
tongue you believe yours, even as it slips
into my dark maw: hold it while you can.

Secrets I savour like a fine old wine
bottled before phylloxera swept through
     the vineyards of the world
and I adore the undiscovered clue,
the mystery unsolved, the lie, the line
a poet forgets, the insult never hurled.

After your truth commissions have wound up
and much redacted, as they had to be
     released their last reports
which will be found to have betrayed the hope
with which they started, it may prove a sort
of comfort, being left alone with me.

The High Possil meteorite, 1804, Scotland. GLAHM:M172

Traces · David Kinloch

They say Mary wept tears at the tomb
door. Until she was addressed by name.
Then there was a muckle flood,
a sea even. This was on Saturday.
The High Possil Meteorite struck Scotland
on a Thursday, another of those prolegomenal
days. Although this chip off a much older block
was tardy to say the least. 4.5 billion years
late, give or take a few. It still had water
in its veins though. Or the traces.
It hit a quarry – divine bingo! – nudging
aside – explosively by all accounts –
the detritus from local slavers' mansions.
Now, it's a quiet thing; you widny greet owre it.

Monument dedicated to the High Possil meteorite at place of fall
(© Creative Commons)

Vertebrata (Knorpelfische) – Rays · Ian Stephen

What lies within is out.
Intricacies bled in ink
offset to cloth.
A skeleton splayed as
a shark with wings –
equipped to run the ground.

Explorer or printer
chavin for replication
knowing we'll never measure up
to delicacy beyond dentistry
of fossil lines in stone as in
'The Bearsden Shark' – mouth plates too.

Mold or cast, relief or intaglio,
we need to borrow
mechanical structures from the dead.
Bones as still as the arms of forceps
which could only circle life
when we upped the anti
to the septic.

Our responses amount to
a pibroch of Arctic variations
in the hinged barbs of fish-hooks
aye ready to snare on impact.
Down a hemisphere to
compound curves, also still,
in Polynesian variations.

The achieved shapes
as various as ballads
sung over borders.

All of us, white coats or no,
restrained by awe or by
the limits of our dexterity.
We can't match
precision in the catch.
We're lost in the looking,
more so, in the trying.

Fish-hook (Matau), 1700–83, New Zealand. GLAHM:E.652

Kava bowl (Nelcau-Amon), collected on Aneityum in 1859. GLAHM:E.406

Note: Nelcau, an ancestral relic and ceremonial vessel from Aneityum Island, Vanuatu, in the Pacific Ocean. It was collected between 1845 and 1859 by the Rev Dr George Turner, who served as a missionary in the South Pacific and presented his collection to The Hunterian in 1860.

The Nelcau at The Hunterian · Hannah Lavery

        Nelcau caught on the screen,
        perfect catch in fraying net.
        We try to return you

He said you were evidence
of how we survived the flood.
Fitted you into a tale he understood,
brought you back, to position you as
a discovery of his missionary zeal. His discovery
of what was already known. A relic already.

I look at you now, virtually, on my screen,
imagine your weight in my hands,
fill you up with more imaginings.
Is this the way of things?

The constant transference.

Does a bowl only contain what it holds?
& what holds? & what could not be held
in his story of you? You are his evidence
we survived the flood & we bring you here
to our lips, to our ears, to our eyes
on a cracked phone screen.

Like a conch shell, I think,
you sing of an old longing.

        The sea that we fished
        still rises, the Gods have left.
        We try to return you.

Francis Campbell Boileau Cadell, *Iona, North End*, c.1917–20. GLAHA:43416

Peploe to Cadell · Ian Stephen

How can you navigate
without knowing it?
How can you be underway but
keel-side up?

But we did sail, through June
from Peploe to Cadell.
Ardalanish shining astern
till we took the dog-legs through
pink to green granite –
Erraid to the Sound of Iona.
Clouds very like the islands under them
as we reached, close, fine, free,
tack to tack till
we were looking up and out that other way
to shale and slate in the low stratus
inches over
or under
Loch na Keal.

FOUR

CREATION: WOMBS OF LIFE & DEATH

The child in the womb in its natural situation, c. 1750. GLAHM:125630

Uterus in the Fifth Month Opened, Showing the Membranes and the enclosed foetus · Samuel Tongue

You haven't changed. Every time I visit,
it's the same scene, repeated. Uterine membranes
as stage curtains held open in a wet preparation,
and here you are, a cidered fruit, performing
all the difficulty in just getting born. I would say
forever but that's the conservationist's lie.
The day the resurrection men brought
you to Hunter's back door, bellied inside an unnamed
woman, dead and pliable, his observations were sensible:
the inflations, the amniotic flavours,
soakings, dryings, injections of wax,
dissection as a menu to be worked through.

This morning the sonographer ran a wand
across and around my wife's glorious belly, gelled
and cool, and here you are, a straight-to-tv
movie: whole and echo; parcel and gift;
body and body. Everything is changing.
Between us, we gaze through the skin's gauze,
the fatty comfort, and guess at the threads
and cloudy formations scudding across the screen.
The midwife measures from cranium to tail,
working out how many days you have left
and everything pulses around this visible point
where hope might stick, gummy and raw and now.

In Utero · Anne Frater

Tha fios againn cò esan.
Esan air a chlàradh –
ainm agus ìomhaigh –
a bhathais air reothadh
ann am masg ciùin a' bhàis.

Tha fios againn cò esan.
Esan a gheàrr i
gus faighinn thugad-sa;
mìorbhail na beatha air a rùsgadh dhuinn
ged nach do dh'fhosgail e dhutsa.

Tha fios againn cò esan.
Esan a chòmhdaich sibh le plèistear
às an do rinn e
ìomhaigh
dathach, luaidhe
ded neo-bhreith
agus a bàis.

Chan d' fhuair màthair no pàist
ainm no urram
ach na dh'innseadh dè a bh' unnaibh
seach cò sibh.

An obair mhòr aigesan
ga moladh
gun ghuth air a saothair-se
sa call.

Chan e dealbh a tha seo
ìomhaigh ann am frèama
ach tàmailt air dithis
a bha beò
gus nach do rugadh tusa.

Ach seo sibh,
air ur cur far comhair
mar obair ealain ann an galaraidh,
dealbh neo-bhreith
agus bàs –
mar nach biodh unnaibh
ach dealbh neo-bheò Pheploe:
sìtheanan pinc agus dearg
a' fosgladh
ann a' bhàsa
air a' bhòrd.

In Utero · Anne Frater

We know who he was.
He is recorded –
name and image –
the face on him frozen
in the peaceful mask of death.

We know who he was.
Him who cut her open
to get to you;
the miracle of life peeled open for us
although it didn't open for you.

We know who he was.
He who covered you in plaster
to make a colourful
leaden
image
of your non-birth
and her death.

Neither mother nor child
named or respected;
we know only what you were
not who.

His great work
praised;
with no word of her labour
and loss.

This is not a picture
an image in a frame
but an insult to two
who lived
until you weren't born.

Yet here you are,
presented to us
like artworks in a gallery,
a picture of non-birth
and death –
as if you were another
Peploe still-life:
pink and red flowers
opening
in a vase
on the table.

There's a Hole in the News
the Size of Poetry · Jane Goldman

(after Anne Boyer)

gravid uterus wet
specimen

gravid uterus plaster
cast

gravid uterus lead
cast

morphologies of parts
of a woman dead
in pregnancy
in the ninth month

the child in the womb
in its natural situation
made of lead

full of lead

this gravid uterus
(already a grave)
occupies

a large portion
of the abdominal
cavity

liver stomach spleen
visible

brown coils of small
intestine
visible

(weapons)

above and left of
the uterine
fundus

lower anterior
abdominal
wall div
ided
down
to the
symphysis pubis

swollen labia majora
visible

swollen labia minora
visible

clitoris in the midline

(a weapon)

upper thighs tran
sected

      expose
d cut shaft of
femur and sur
      rounding
muscles give
a butchered
effect

a butchered
effect

is this real
this is real

give me gas and air
give me gas and air

is this real
this is real

as real as
the palest
stone

and babies
(question mark)

and babies
(full stop)

and babies
came this
real way

without anaesthetic
without incubators

without critical
infrastructures

and babies
(question mark)

and babies
(full stop)

full of lead

blasted through a hole
in the news
the size of poetry

Unit tray of Blood-red longhorn beetles
(Anastranglia sanguinolenta), ENTO:25/BR/144A.

Insects in the woods of Caledon · Alan Riach

Blera fallax goes for the heartwood –
What nature creates we recreate, a rot hole full of
Sawdust for the young,
Nutrient soup for the larvae
For baby hoverflies, their bottoms vivid red in life,
        the pigments fade
When the creatures are here, on the pin.

From Nethybridge, beetles, dried, preserved,
Blood-red longhorns (*Anastrangalia sanguinolenta*),
        Scots Pine specialists.
Their grubs nestled in burrows in Scots pines a couple of
        hundred years ago.
Other similar longhorn beetles, from the same taxonomic family,
        the Cerambycidae,
Perfectly preserved intact for plus 3,000 years in bog oak.
Cognate and contemporary and reaching long before
Beetles from Egyptian tombs:
        so long, in good conditions,
endures the exoskeleton.

But the living beetle's pedigree is millions of years.
        Their dried remains hold firm,
Longhorn beetles here in The Hunterian, hard shells,
        chitinous armour,
Even dismembered, fragmented by rough handling, crossed
Two centuries and more, to here, close pinned in the Collection.
Their larva feed on dead wood, adults
On the hogweed blooms, other umbelliferas and Rowan. We might
Give ourselves time, to pause on that. The longhorn beetles'

Ancestors go back a hundred million years & more,
    started to diversify
As and when the land plants did. And the blood red longhorn
    beetles, living,
Also have their preference, good rotten heartwood & stumps.

Then the mountain bumblebees, bilberry bees, or
    Blaeberry bees (in Scots),
Bombus monticola, feeding in the understory, at higher levels,
    and in cooler places.
Little flying teddy bears, cold climate bees, their thick fur
    furry warm, their wings
To be uncoupled as & when, not flying but warming
Themselves, generating heat. And their predators,
    the bumblebee robberfly,
Take them down on the wing, inject them with their neurotoxins,
Balance the books, survive.

At ground level, as you ascend, at a certain height,
At a certain warmth of temperature, the murmuring of bees,
    the gentle murmurations,
The quiet level sloping floor of susurration, stops. Too high,
    too cold,
Above a certain balance, these things cease,
    these creatures do not.

And not in the forest but over on the coasts, on the machair
By the Hebridean seas, the great yellow bumblebee pertains.

The Kentish Glory Moth was lost in England, unseen there since 1969, or 70,
But in Scotland, the generations didn't stop, lived on
In the birches of the Caledon.
The forest kept them, balanced,
In its various complications.

In the Black Wood of Rannoch Moor, for the bordered white moth there,
The species interactions are all right. But caterpillar-hungry,
It makes sufficient problems for the industry of forestry:
The balance isn't there. Its appetite is big plantations.
No problem in the Woods of Caledon, where what remains, complexity, survives,
But strict commercial purpose, favours a conformity.

Below all these, the wood ants: *Formica aquilonia,* the genus,
Scottish wood ants & exsecta, dark abdomens, reddish forebodies,
But these are more than simply birdfood, they are a keystone species,
Regulating populations, pests, the creatures that these creatures feed on.
They eat the insects insects otherwise eat, all of them keystone,
Strata intersecting, sloping, interleaving, locking, loving
What they are, and eat. And then become.
Honeydew from aphids,
Protecting the aphids, milking them like cows,
            looking after them.
Ants dispersing seeds recycle nutrients, make shelter for
So many other types of tiny things.

And those shining guest ants, tiniest of all, found in the centres
Of hollow sticks, which clamber onto other ants,
                begging them for food,
Producing a distinctive smell, not for blending in
                but to clearly mark
Their own distinctiveness, and thus, make the appeal, to recognise
Their place as something else, within this world of minuscule
Diversities, extending far as all the world can be, opposing
Uniformity, and all its cruel enforcements, endorsing
What we now know nature is, and shows us, and corrects us with.

Drawer of British moths and caterpillars including the Bordered white moth or Pine looper *(Bupalus piniaria)* on the left, ENTO:25/BR/144A.

FIVE

POINTS OF VANTAGE

John Cunningham, *Wet Haystack*, 1963–65. © the artist's estate. GLAHA:43448

The Trees · Alan Riach

This bit of the forest has haunted my dreams
For a long time. Nineteen sixty-three, or four, and
I would be six, or seven, seeing it then for the first time
Only once, you see things for the first time only
Once. After that, repeats, returns, the little clutch of company
Of trees in middle distance – approaching? Or retreating,
Beckoning you, come forward, come in, come into our shelter,
The trees. Negotiate wet haystacks, hard grass, hay stalks high,
And then be among us. A part of the forest. But hold back,
Take a full view: bright-coloured flowers in the foreground,
Blue skies, warm brightness, high space, far above. The trees
Come no closer. Nor do they retreat. But their presence looms
Permanent, there, and that fixture, security, 's right.
It means that your mind can walk through them, or pause,
Before, or look down from the clouds to imagine them, there.
Or just watch them, from this, the appropriate distance.

Alan Davie, *Sea Devil's Watchtower,* 1960. © The Estate of Alan Davie. All rights reserved. DACS 2024. GLAHA:43459

In Alan Davie's Paintings · Liz Lochhead

An ee
an open ee
whit seems but an ashet o
bools and penny-cookies mak an arabesque
an arra-heid edder frae ablow it gaes serpent-slinkan
yont the picture frame.
a jazz o bird-heids, herts, peeries, playin cairts
the crescent mune –
a the shapes and symbols frae
ankh to ziggurat, corbie-steppit.
whiles a rattle-stane blatter
whiles a hurly-gush o colour – wow
this lovely lowe o cramasie, soy-saft,
noo the reid, reid, reid o thunnercups,
a braid and tappietourie swag o emerant
yallochie
blae.

Note: Since its purchase in 1963, the Hunterian Art Gallery has kept on permanent display *Sea Devil's Watchtower*, a large (H 122 & W 154) oil-on-hardboard Alan Davie painting from 1960. The above poem references even more oft-repeated motifs from the great Scottish artist's work of this period than are contained in this particular example, but in entirely typical fashion the grace-notes of cramasie (crimson), reid (scarlet), emerant (emerald), and blae (blue) counter the triumphant towering trumpet blast of yallochie (yellow).

Figure of Buddha, Myanmar. GLAHM:E.260

John Anderson's Buddha · Colin Bramwell

The perfect antiquated symmetry
betrays his being in this place and time.
On the leaf behind the form, a Byzantine
halo cast in bronze sets daylight free

to exhaust the eye – likewise that dark grey
underwhelms you with its own shine, turning
all embossed courtiers into the one burning,
dulling block of not-quite-black. Flautists play

their silent airs, some dance on smoke or cloud.
If you shut your own eyes too, the overloud
museum will crackle in your ear like fire

and his advice will flare and catch and sing.
The poor will take what they can from the poorer –
you can't change that. You won't change anything.

Buddha's hand, Myanmar. GLAHM:106713

James McNeill Whistler, *Brown and Gold: Self-Portrait*, 1895–1900. GLAHA:46376

JMW · Ian Stephen

It's what you can nearly see –
the hull under suggested sailcloth,
the fan of fingers, a fan itself,
the hem over bulge of boot.
You get the stances.
You wonder at the not-quite-red,
flower or pom or what
is left in the figure's wake –
a possibility of glow
out of scrupulous charcoal.

His own portrait – another arrangement
but can the self really be
skinny as a waif in a long coat?
Something like a reveal
in his organisation of
legs, arms, miraculous hands.

SIX

ITEMS

Head of a Young Woman · Lynn Davidson
after Alison Watt

How does the face move and yet hold still?
Thoughts seem to lift into it, like
birds, and

her inward-looking eyes (so worked)
follow those thought-birds across
fields and towns, coming and going from

their winter home – glossy drape of mud flat
and river mouth, the webbed print
the shallow water swallows.

Late afternoon sun, bare
as a neck, illuminates the room. The young head
achieves its form and through it

the old forms rise (as they do). Outside the window
some creature barks or coughs and
the day folds its light

like linen. There is
a pouring down of dusk, in which, I imagine,
she goes, leaves the portrait room,

the young woman, her coat, an exchange,
a smile, a rearrangement. In the sweet present
her body turns like a river,

her eyes suddenly looking for the usual things –
a bus, a friend, her flat,
a window, its catch, the evening coming in.

Alison Watt, *Head of a Young Woman,* 1994. © Alison Watt. GLAHA:55685

A Face On The Move · Jane Goldman

After Lynn Davidson, after Alison Watt

so left-sided like

a shift in a cloth

nose folded into

one single nostril

so left-sided or

self-portrait in

right profile as

river mouth at low

tide hers a shallow

water swallowed by

a nipped purse

button-lipped over

a lost word such

a sweet presence

hangs with a word

out here lost in space

space of body turn

her one ear visible

tuning in over

grey pastel waves

and the evening

coming in over

her chin

Model 'Newcomen' steam engine, 1722–60. GLAHM:C29

After Newcomen's Engine · Lindsay Macgregor

Have we forgotten the point of ignition
    after we turned ourselves on?
  Not the tip of a lit cigarette that has fallen
   to tinder the duff desecration of flowers
 in a twenty-first century west-facing forest
    far to the left of our capital city but
   the flickering thought of a profit
  burning to bloom from the furnace
   of Scottish enlightenment,
   us as upstanding versions of creed,
     lying still in the silence of street-names
      and statuary, driven as national inventors
   with a passion for power looms,
  pistons and spinning mules, thrilled
at the prospect of sweetening
  Greenock and Leith while the red lion
  rampant is reaping his fortune
   from steam locomotion and grief.
   Have we forgotten so soon?

Sir Francis Legatt Chantrey, *James Watt (1736–1819)*. GLAHA:44337

The Statue of James Watt · Bashabi Fraser

A pensive scholar sits relaxed and preoccupied,
concentrating on innovative technology that would transform
lives forever, contributing to civilization's panting progress,
propelled by an energy to ease travel and production
for the benefit of burgeoning trade, controlled by the
power of those who generated wealth through harnessing
broken human bodies.

Countless bodies were captured, chained, transported,
bought and sold in the very markets that thrived on
their backbreaking labour, extracted by brutality.
The fortunate ones died in that dark passage in the bowels
Of unbreathable, crowded cavities, thrown unceremoniously
Overboard to feed the sharks who followed the sharklike
Owners on dark voyages.

The captives couldn't breathe, praying silently for air and freedom
As their descendants do today across the Atlantic,
        their prayers ignored.
The voices of the past, muffled or muted by misery and mutilation
Come back to haunt us in a populace united beyond colour –
To rummage through the rubble of human destruction, to uncover
The truth behind a direct beneficiary of an unholy alliance
In a new resurrection.

John Knox, *The Nelson Monument Struck by Lightning*, 1817–21. GLAHA:43921

Òraid air an dàrna, air neo math dh'fhaoidte an treas nochdadh, de Cholbh Nelson · Pàdraig MacAoidh

Glòr thar chàich dha Nelson is Ìmpireachd
ghlòrmhor Bhreatainn, nach tèid am bualadh
gu sìorruidh bràth; thar Dhia agus dealanach
dìobhalta Aige; thar chrìochan Ùr-
Clasaigeach an landskipp; gu h-àraid
thar sibhse, a' ghràisg, a' màirnealachd

gun fhurtachd aig bonn an deilbh. Gum bi
bùth ann a reiceas cairtean-puist cuingichte
de thiotag mhìorbhailleach Knox – Dia
agus Tìr aonaichte mu dheireadh thall –
agus a reiceas cuideachd an dèidh mi-thuigse
ann an ainm, lethbhreacan dhen leabhar First

Blast of the Trumpet Against the Monstrous
Regiment of Women. Gum bi sibh
a' coimhead air obair Knox, sibhse a tha
cumhachdach, agus faireachdainn co-dhiù
beagan de mhì-chofhurtachd. Thèid rudan
ath-thogail. 'S dòcha gu bheil rudeigin fhathast

a' dabhdail a dh'ìonnsaigh Lèanag Ghlaschu
air feasgar close: chan e buileach aimsir
taps aff a th'ann, ach faisg air, ga gealladh.

Speech on the second, or maybe third, unveiling of Nelson's Column · Peter Mackay

Glory be, above all, to Nelson and
the British Empire that will never
be struck down; above God even
and his diabolic lightning; above
the limits of neo-Classical
landskipps; above you scruff milling
disconsolate in your bottom corners.

May the gift shop for ever more sell
limited edition postcards of Knox's
glorious moment, of God and country
finally united; and also sell,
after a nominal misunderstanding,
paperback copies of John Knox's First

Blast of the Trumpet Against the Monstrous
Regiment of Women. May you look
on Knox's work you mighty,
and feel at least slight discomfort. Things
can always be rebuilt, better. Something
might still be slouching towards Glasgow Green

on a slightly close afternoon in spring –
when it's not quite taps aff weather yet,
but threatening to be.

John Scougall, *John Knox (1505–72)*, 1660–1738. GLAHA:44246

Mittens · Em Strang

On our own, we're nothing.
Inside the quiet pelt of us,
the spirit-hands of humans
wave beyond time and snow.

We sleep in a cabinet of knowing,
a small, glass bed for beloveds,
barely touching yet intimate
in the way ice is intimate with snow.

We might have melted by now,
rotted, or been eaten by wolves,
but no: here behold our selves,
untouched, at rest, de facto,

with beginnings that begin again
with each viewer, each pair of visitor eyes,
each heart beating to our stitching
across the vast tundra of the familiar.

We are whole beings. We've made
ourselves whole by giving ourselves
away, a gift we learnt from
the deer, their seasoned surrender.

The world cannot reach us now. Now
we understand the past is the same
bright burden as the future – a child's
pointing thumb heralding something

none of us can comprehend.
These careful stitches keep us intact,
shape us, make us 'mittens'
and the rest is miracle, unfathomable.

Who made us? Ask the snow.
Ask the North Wind. Ask the wide land
of the Huron-Wendat. Then rest with us
inside the not-knowing forever.

Mittens, 1750–1800, Native American/Canadian First
Nations, Huron-Wendat, North America. GLAHM:E.105

Woven bag, 1800–60, New Caledonia. GLAHM:E.411/1

A bag for magic stones · Richard Price

I wanted to kill the man
so one yam-stone let me walk
out of my skin
and it's only a few miles to his home.

What's wrong with her?
It all began with smiles and smirks,
with 'making love' –
risking wrath and reputation
for tenderness and touch.
Now it's duty, frequent. And still no child.
This stone says, Soon.

Here's the one for the eels – a growing family will need to eat!

And the last of the yam-stones is for us all –
for more yams of course (though the number of stones
must not grow).

May there be a rich harvest.

SEVEN

ARTICLES OF FAITH

Duncan Shanks, *Fragments of Memory,* early 1990s.
© Duncan Shanks. GLAHA:56537

Source · Liz Lochhead

The sun had to blaze, the rain to pour down
and the wind to blow wild.
– Duncan Shanks, 2015

He says (does this man
who believes *the artist's work*
should always speak for itself) that he
never *paints a scene*.
He asserts he has no urge to paint a landscape, but
to paint the experience of being out in that landscape.
He never goes out with *an idea*
but goes out with as little as
an empty mind
an empty page
perhaps four or five
seemingly random (though they won't be) Rembrandt pastels
a 2 or 4B pencil
a stick of compressed charcoal.
See how the moment he puts a single stroke to paper
any daft, irrelevant illusion of a border
between the figurative and the abstract dissolves?

I've always got to make marks.

Does not have to be
the Sturm und Drang drama of Corra Linn, but
something
has to happen.
A ripple, a pebble, a bird's skull, a dead field mouse,
a brassy shaft of light through cloud,

the mixed blessing of a downpour –
even in the highest, brightest blue of day
a sliver or a sudden
round white moon might intervene.

He has to go out to go in.

Not ours to know
anything of the alternating frustration and flow
of his subsequent
in-studio, in paint, struggle
to retrieve, translate landscape into mindscape,
to marry layer upon layer of deep memory
with glancing moments of specific grace
and create his wordless poetry of place.

Note: In 2013 the great Scottish landscape painter Duncan Shanks (born 1937) gifted to The Hunterian well over one hundred of his sketchbooks, a (so far) lifetime's work containing over six and a half thousand drawings, very many of them responses to the intimate, immediate local terrain around the home and garden in the Upper Clyde village of Crossford where he and his wife had already been living and working for over half a century. More than a decade on there's been neither slowing down nor any diminishing of his powers, with a fresh and vital solo exhibition from Shanks approximately every two years.

In 2015, to celebrate the completion of the massive task of photographing, cataloguing, launching as an online resource, this wonderful acquisition, the Hunterian published a scholarly, informative and lavishly illustrated book alongside their major exhibition (based around a mere thirty of these sketchbooks) entitled *The Poetry of Place: Duncan Shanks's Sketchbooks and the Upper Clyde.*

Duncan Shanks, *Looking up a Gulley and Scree, Tinto,* late 1990s. © Duncan Shanks. GLAHA:56465/71

Still Life and Rosechatel wi You · Lesley Benzie

The licht shimmys lithesome fae
Cadell's Rosechatel Bordeaux,
the wine gless draws the ee
      as yours drink me in.

The cheir, bricht reid, colour saturate, still
life intoxicates, bleed rises tae flush oor chiks,
seams o heat course throwe oor veins, till
ah cin feel the very banes o you. An in the fine
brush strokes memorise the rhythm o yer spine
as oor bodies tell ane anither the aulest
      story o aa time,

for wint o the wurds unspoken. Denyin
that we've aaready uncovered depths
beyond the duck-egg cover o this buik,
read atween its lines enough tae consider
whither tae replenish this cup o vintage teal
      that oors micht yet rin ower.

If nae, fur this backdrop o Prussian Blue,
an oor ideals disillusioned like characters
in a Chekhov play, though like this pintin
ah'm Scottish throwe an throwe an
Scottish bleed belies yer English tongue,

we've cairret a hail warld o complex livin
      been judged an yet misjudged

an contrary tae this vibrant bergamot
kept close the black ae hairtbrakk,
held oor een firm tae the palest yalla meen,
caad-throwe fur reasons or mebbe jist excuses

    nae tae open up again
    tae luv
    the wurkins o pure airt.

Francis Campbell Boileau Cadell, *Still Life and Rosechatel,* 1924. GLAHA:43420

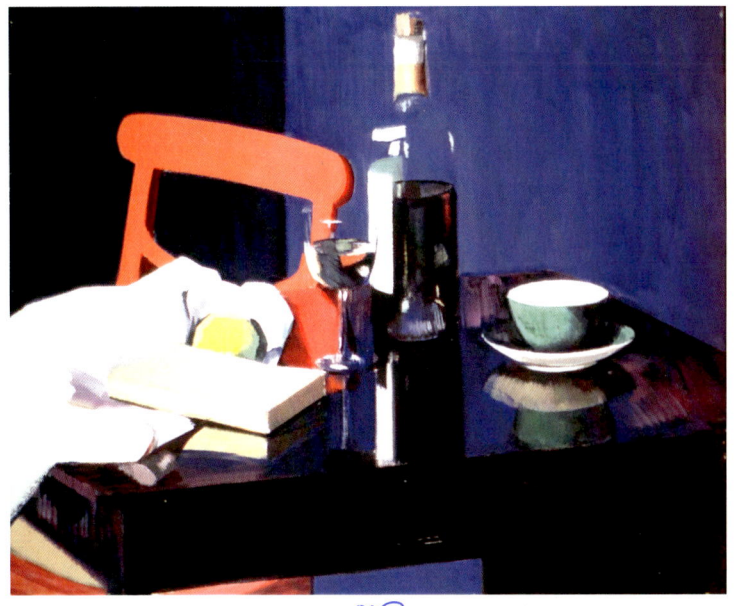

Tombstone of Flavius Lucianus, AD 142–180,
Bar Hill Roman Fort, Scotland. GLAHM:F.36

Inscriptions · Gerrie Fellows

Lettered sandstone
patterned to a broken edge
DEO MARti CAMVLO
a prayer inscribed in a second language
remnant   among cracked open
            fragments
come to sight in quarried earth

From a courtyard well   coins and finger rings
Rome's stamp   *HADRIANVS AVGVSTVS*
given up   to a place with its own weather
          filled as the well itself with ghosts
          named
                 and nameless

      bones, human   *phalanges*
NW corner of the Praetentura, refuse pit 1

The tombstone of a soldier
inscribed   *to the spirits of the departed*
FLAvivs LVCIANVS

The tombstone of a soldier
eroded   without inscription

forgotten
        guessed at
               come to light

among hazel twigs and local earth
all that continues
paved-over mavericks the laverock sings over

Egidius van Tilborch, *Interior with a Music Party,* 1650–1700. GLAHA:43829

A mass-produced Neapolitan mandolin.

Chaff · Peter McCarey

People tell me things, for I forget.
Women come to me because I fear them.
Light and tight I am as any
Junk in the belly of the loft –
A Neapolitan mandolin, its neck
The yoke, its bowl one pan of the scales that weigh
Or sift your grief and craft.

Finer instruments absorb the merit of the player;
It throbs in them until they lie, beyond music and its tension,
Under glass. But mine is a wooden lollipop, economic
Refugee, merchandise from pre-war hits on shellac
Seventy-eights. It's suffered bad beginners, broken bridges,
Accepted wedding gigs to pay reminders, never balked
At a fiddler's bidding. Till it's jiggered:

A curl to the lip of the soundhole twists the fretboard out of true,
Like the time a bluetit smacked into the glass;
It lay in shock, it lay in state,
The neighbours' children paying their respects.
Neighbourhood crows in Crombies bide their time;
What did you make of the bit about fearing women?
Don't get it. Ask the busker. He'll probably say he cannae mind.

Articles of Faith · David Kinloch

The Voice is crabbit from the outset.
'A': 'has too many different significations',
'In Galic is called for *Ailm*.' 'A', it stutters,
'his, her, it's', or 'an ascent, hill or promontery';
'improperly', it girns, 'A: improperly
a sign of the present and future tense.
'Improperly, a sign of the vocative'.
It should be written 'o', as in '*o dhia*'.
It is unwilling to commit itself to English,
reluctant to unsnarl its roots in ancient 'elm'.

As a young teacher I used to pat my dictionary in class
to bolster my authority. But I knew about its strained
bravado, the lunar landscapes of conjecture,
bushfires of quotations, starry asterisks that led nowhere;
and how a single definition could be a poem.

The rough breath of etymologies
stalked me through a labyrinth of entries.
Here, the wreck ground of language,
backstairs words that peter out
in goat tracks stumbling from a swooning
mind; the outlines of mountaintops
sprouting autonomously from sketchy air;
Minoan shards, ceramic guesswork.

There is too much of 'Ailm' this one says.
Yet when I moved to declutter shelves
of dictionaries, my mother stopped me.

'Give one of them to me', she said,
patting and patting. She keeps it beside
the phone. When was the Medusa born?

I call my mother and listen to her snakes
and ladders game with words: one rung, two,
eight sometimes, and then she slithers
down among the million mouthing heads,
her voice a wrecked 'O', an improper
vocative. 'A', she mouths, and again 'a',
that awkward indefinite article
with which we begin and end.

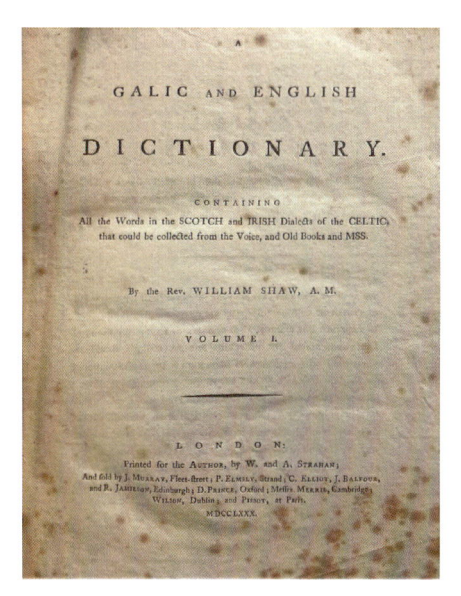

William Shaw, *A Galic and English dictionary* (Sp Coll Hunterian EE.1.3-4), 1780. By permission of University of Glasgow Archives and Special Collections.

Alexander Moffat, *Àird an Dòchais / The Compass of Hope* (detail). © Alexander Moffat.

The Water of Hope · Alan Riach

When clear water runs
From the well in the mountain
Marked by the Celtic design,
The patchwork quilt of languages,
That make the earth a habitable globe,
(Their colours of such designations,
Their parts of the planet define),
Will welcome its music & movement:
A channel of tunes in a whole world of learning.

When the children play fiddle & clarsach,
And sing to the teacher's direction,

When the colours are such as enhance
Bright minds & the deepest reflection,
The learning begins.
                      What it brings us,
The water, the colours, the shapes & the sounds,
Is a play to be in, to be part of
But also to witness & watch.
                           The curves,
The circle, the cube, the straight line
And the crooked, sign languages
And Glaschu, home of such collections
Of good hopes, these prospects:
Aspirations. Independence.

Biographies

Mungo Campbell was the Deputy Director of The Hunterian at the University of Glasgow until his retirement in 2024. He was the commissioning editor of *The Hunterian Poems: An Anthology of Poems to Paintings from the collection of The Hunterian at the University of Glasgow* (2015) and *The Hunterian Museum Poems: A History of the World in Objects and Poems* (2017).

Lesley Benzie is Aberdonian but has made the West Coast her home. An editor at *Mxogyny Magazine* comparing her to Burns, prompted Lesley's comment: 'I'm blessed with a quarter of the number of children and have indulged in much less philandering'. She is the author of *Sewn Up* and *Fessen/Reared* and a contributor to the collaborative collections, *Wanderlust Women* (2021), *Wanderlust Women: Extra Baggage* (2023) and *Norlan Lichts* (2022). instagram.com/lesleybenzie/

Colin Bramwell is from the Black Isle. He was the runner up for the 2020 Edwin Morgan Prize and won the 2018 John Dryden Translation Competition. His poems and translations have been published in *PN Review*, *Poetry Review*, *Magma*, *The London Magazine* and elsewhere.

Lynn Davidson's memoir *Do you still have time for chaos?* was published by Te Herenga Waka University Press, Wellington, in 2024. Her latest poetry collection *Islander* was published by Shearsman Books, and Te Herenga Waka University Press in 2019. She has had a Hawthornden Fellowship and a Bothy Project Residency. Lynn calls Aotearoa New Zealand and Scotland home. Lynn is a member of 12, a collective of women poets based in Scotland.

Gerrie Fellows has published seven collections of poetry including *Uncommon Place*, poems about Scotland and the nature of place. After contributing to earlier Hunterian anthologies, she became preoccupied with exploring the museum's collection; these poems were published as *Shadow Box* (Shearsman, 2023). A New Zealander by birth, Gerrie has lived in Scotland since the early '80s.

Bashabi Fraser, CBE, HonFASL, is an award-winning poet, children's writer, translator, editor and academic. She is Professor Emerita of English and Creative Writing at Edinburgh Napier University and Co-Founder and Director of the Scottish Centre of Tagore Studies (ScoTs). Bashabi has written and edited 25 books, published several articles/chapters in international journals/books and has been widely anthologised as a poet. She is on the Editorial Board of several international journals and is Chief Editor of *Gitanjali and Beyond*. Bashabi is a Royal Literary Fund Fellow, an Honorary Fellow at CSAS, University of Edinburgh and has been declared an Outstanding Woman of Scotland by the Saltire Society in 2015.

Anne C Frater was born in Stornoway (Steòrnabhagh), in Lewis in the Western Isles (na h-Eileanan Siar) and brought up in the village of Upper Bayble (Pabail Uarach) in the district of Point. Her first collection, *Fo'n t-Slige* (*Under the Shell*) was published in 1995, and her second, *Cridhe Creige*, in 2017.

Jane Goldman is Reader in English Literature and Creative Writing at Glasgow University and likes anything a word can do. Her poems have appeared in numerous magazines and anthologies including *The Hunterian Museum Poems* (2015). She is author of the pamphlet *Border Thoughts* (2014), and *SEKXPHRASTIKS*

(2021), her debut collection: 'a provocative and joyous menagerie' (Lila Matsumoto). *Catullus 64* (2023) is her scandalous translation of the Latin poet Catullus's satirical mini-epic. She is a member of 12, a collective of women poets based in Scotland, contributing to *Spaces Open* (2023) and *Pink Witch* (2024). She is co-author, with Colin Herd, Nicky Melville, Iain Morrison and Maria Sledmere, of *not just A NY QUINCUNX* (2024), a whimsical document of five Scottish poets let loose in New York city.

David Kinloch was born and brought up in Glasgow. His latest book is *Greengown: New and Selected Poems* (Carcanet) and he is Emeritus Professor of Poetry at the University of Strathclyde. A founder and past Chair of The Edwin Morgan Trust, he received a Cholmondeley Award in 2022 in recognition of his work to date.

Hannah Lavery was Edinburgh Makar 2021-24. Her poetry pamphlet, *Finding Seaglass* was published by Stewed Rhubarb and followed by her debut collection, *Blood Salt Spring* (Polygon, 2022). *The Drift*, her autobiographical lyric play toured with the National Theatre of Scotland. Her play *Lament for Sheku Bayoh* premiered at the Edinburgh International Festival in 2020. She is an associate artist with the National Theatre of Scotland and has written for BBC Radio Four, Lyceum Theatre, Pitlochry Theatre, Northern Stage, Traverse Theatre and various publications including *The Scotsman*, *The Guardian* and *Gutter Magazine*. In 2022, she launched with Scottish Feminist Theatre Company, Stellar Quines, a feminist arts podcast, Quines Cast, which she co-hosts with Caitlin Skinner.

Liz Lochhead was the Scots Makar from 2011 till 2016, when she was also awarded the Queen's Gold Medal for Poetry. The recently published *A Handsel, New & Collected Poems* spans the more than fifty years since her popular debut collection *Memo for Spring* in 1972. As a dramatist, the best-known of her original plays are Blood and Ice (1982) *Mary Queen of Scots Got Her Head Chopped Off* (1987) and *Perfect Days* (2000). Her biographical *Thon Man Moliere* (2016) is about that French genius of comedy whose three masterpieces *Le Tartuffe*, *Le Misanthrope* and *L'Ecole des Femmes* have all been adapted by Lochhead into rhyming couplets in Scots – *Tartuffe*, *Miseryguts* and *Educating Agnes* respectively. Her versions of some of the Greek tragedies, Euripides's *Medea* (2000) – revised by her in 2023 as the National Theatre of Scotland's major production at that year's Edinburgh International Festival) – and also Sophocles' Oedipus Rex and *Antigone* have been linked by fragments either ancient or invented, into one single epic drama under the title *Thebans* (2003).

Marcas Mac an Tuairneir is a poet, singer-songwriter, translator and editor based in Edinburgh. His fourth collection, *Polaris*, was shortlisted for the Saltire Society's Scottish Poetry Book of the Year Award. He received the Wigtown Gaelic Poetry Prize in 2017 and a National Gaelic Award for Arts and Culture in 2023.

'S ann à Leòdhas a tha **Pàdraig MacAoidh**, agus chaidh dà leabhar leis fhoillseachadh le Acair, *Gu Leòr* agus *Nàdur De*, agus pamflaid, *From another island*, le Clutag Press. Tha e a' fuireach ann an Dun Èideann.

Peter Mackay has two collections with Acair, *Galore* and *Some Kind of*, and a pamphlet, *From another island*, with Clutag Press. Originally from the Isle of Lewis, he now lives in Edinburgh, and works in St Andrews.

Lindsay Macgregor lives in Biggar where she works in Atkinson-Pryce independent bookshop. She has an MLitt in Writing Practice and Study from the University of Dundee. In 2015 she received a Scottish Book Trust New Writers' Award and in 2017, a Hawthornden Fellowship. *The Weepers* was published by Calder Wood Press in 2015 and *Desperate Fishwives* by Molecular Press in 2022.

Peter McCarey was born in Paisley and brought up in Glasgow, taking degrees from Oxford in Russian and French and Glasgow in Russian and Scottish literature. He lives in Geneva, where for many years he was the World Health Organisation Head of Language Services. His poetry is in *Collected Contraptions* (2011) and *The Syllabary* (2023, online), an epic of 2,772 individual poems. The proceedings of a symposium of international experts he convened to discuss an 'impossible pandemic' were published as *Petrushka* (2017), which the *London Review of Books* called 'one of the strangest and best books' of the year.

Jeda Pearl is a Scottish Jamaican writer. In 2022, she was shortlisted for the Sky Arts RSL Award and longlisted for the Women Poets' Prize. Her poems and stories appear in art installations and several anthologies. Jeda's debut poetry collection is *Time Cleaves Itself* (Peepal Tree Press, 2024). Find her online: @JedaPearl / jedapearl.com.

Richard Price moves comfortably between prose, lyricism and the avant-garde as an influential figure in the literary movement which he himself coined 'Informationist poetry' (which included Peter McCarey and Alan Riach). He has written fiction, collaborated with sculptors, digital artists, photographers and musicians. Born in 1966, he grew up in Renfrewshire, began writing poetry at the age of 14, trained as a journalist at Napier

College, Edinburgh, before taking a degree in English and Librarianship at the University of Strathclyde. His poetry is in *Lucky Day* (2005), *Green Fields* (2007), *Small World* (2012), *Moon for Sale* (Carcanet, 2017), *The Owner of the Sea: Three Inuit Stories Retold* (Carcanet, 2021) and *Late Gifts* (2023)

John Purser is an award-winning composer, writer and musicologist. His books of poetry include *There Is No Night* and *This Much Endures*. He is a Researcher at Sabhal Mòr Ostaig, the Gaelic College on the Island of Skye, where he lives and crofts with his American wife, Barbara. www.johnpurser.net

Samuel Reilly is currently researching Nigerian art in Glasgow's museums for his PhD at the University of St Andrews, with a particular focus on the career of Frank Willett, the first professional director of the Hunterian and an expert on Nigerian art. His writing on art has been published in *Apollo*, *ArtReview*, *Frieze*, *Prospect*, *The Telegraph* and the *Financial Times*, among other publications.

Alan Riach is a poet and Professor of Scottish Literature at Glasgow University. Poetry books include *The MacDiarmid Memorandum* (2023), *The Winter Book* (2017) and *Homecoming* (2009). *The Times Literary Supplement* named *Arts of Resistance* (2008) 'a landmark book'. *The Times* described his critical overview *Scottish Literature: An Introduction* (2022) as 'magisterial'.

Stewart Sanderson is an award-winning poet based in Glasgow. His two pamphlets – *Fios* (2015) and *An Offering* (2018) – were both published by Tapsalteerie, as was his first full-length collection, *The Sleep Road* (2021). He is currently working on a new book of poems, forthcoming with Tapsalteerie in 2025, whose themes include the redemptive possibilities of chance procedures, the weather and the parallels between archaeology and writing.

Ian Stephen (b.1955) lives on Lewis in the Outer Hebrides. He studied English, Drama and Education at Aberdeen University. After 15 years in the coastguard, he became a full-time writer of poetry, prose and drama in 1995. His work is collected in *Malin, Hebrides, Minches*, with photos by Sam Maynard (1983), *Varying States of Grace* (1989), *Providence II* (1994), *Adrift / Napospas vlnám* (2007) and *Maritime: new and selected poems* (2016). His epic novel *A Book of Death and Fish* appeared in 2014.

Em Strang is a poet, novelist and Royal Literary Fund Fellow. Her writing preoccupations are with nature, spirituality and the masculine. Em has published three collections of poetry with Shearsman (*Bird-Woman*, 2016; *Horse-Man*, 2019; *Firebird*, 2024) and has been shortlisted for the Seamus Heaney Best First Collection Prize, the Ledbury Munthe prize for Best Second Collection, and won the 2017 Saltire Poetry Book of the Year Award. Her first novel, *Quinn*, was shortlisted for the 2019 Fitzcarraldo Editions Novel Prize and was published by Oneworld in 2023. See Em Strang Embodied Poetry: em-strang.co.uk/

Samuel Tongue's collections include *Sacrifice Zones* (Red Squirrel, 2020) and three pamphlets: *The Nakedness of the Fathers* (Broken Sleep, 2022), *Stitch* (Tapsalteerie, 2018), *Hauling-Out* (Eyewear, 2016). Poems have appeared in different places, including *Magma, Poetry Wales, Finished Creatures, Perverse* and *Banshee Lit*; some have been translated into Arabic, Latvian, and Estonian. Samuel is also a winner of a New Writers Award from the Scottish Book Trust.

Stewed Rhubarb is Charlie Roy and
Duncan Lockerbie. We are a small, inclusive
press that champions new, diverse poetry.

www.stewedrhubarb.org

SR
STEWED RHUBARB